ERTÉ
FASHIONS
COLORING BOOK

Rendered by
MARTY NOBLE

DOVER PUBLICATIONS, INC.
Mineola, New York

PUBLISHER'S NOTE

Erté was born Romain de Tirtoff in St. Petersburg, Russia, in 1892 ("Erté" is the French pronunciation of the designer's initials). He did not follow his father, an admiral, into a military career; rather, Erté displayed a talent for sketching as a child and set forth on a different path. In 1912, he left Russia for Paris, where he designed dresses for the couture house of Paul Poiret. Keeping his goal of fashion illustration in mind, he soon saw his work in print in *La Gazette du Bon Ton*, a French fashion magazine. It was his association with *Harper's Bazar*, however, that secured his reputation as a foremost fashion illustrator. Erté produced distinctive covers and illustrations for the magazine for over 20 years, beginning in 1915. He devised seasonal covers celebrating the approaching fashion collections for a time, including the plates on pages 6, 7, 9, 11, and 12. In addition, he applied his artistry to theatrical set designs and costumes—fertile ground for his flamboyant creations. In 1988, two years before his death, he was still designing for the theater (the musical *Stardust*).

The 30 renderings of Erté's designs in this book consist of cover designs and inside illustrations from the early years of the artist's association with *Harper's Bazar*. These plates, ranging from 1915 through 1922, convey the masterful drape of the garments pictured, as well as their intricate ornamentation. Included are a cascade of ribbons enveloping a sinuous dancer [Plate 7]; an immense floral-patterned train encircling a serene figure [Plate 17]; and a flowing paisley cape surrounding its masked wearer [Plate 30]. Some of Erté's favored colors for his creations were pearl gray, mauve, coral, rose, gold, silver, and, of course, black and white. He often employed alternating panels of fabric, woven ribbons, and checkerboard patterns in his costumes. Sable, ermine, mole skin, and beaver fur, as well as precious and semiprecious gems, lent luxury to many of his designs. The plates are arranged in the following manner: Cover designs are grouped together, followed by inside illustrations; each grouping is in chronological order (except for Plate 20, where the later date is used).

Copyright

Copyright © 2003 by Dover Publications, Inc.
All rights reserved.

Bibliographical Note

Erté Fashions Coloring Book is a new work, first published by Dover Publications, Inc., in 2003.

International Standard Book Number: 0-486-43041-3

Manufactured in the United States of America
Dover Publications, Inc., 31 East 2nd Street, Mineola, N.Y. 11501

In this dramatic plate, the mountainous terrain supporting the figure is almost entirely black, shot through with red and gold flames at the bottom; gold lava pours over the crest upon which she perches. A red-crested rooster with gray plumage squawks at the right. The figure herself is white, wrapped in strands of red beads. Her head and the lower part of her face are wrapped in lavender star-studded swirls, and her immediate background is a paler shade of lilac. [Cover, January 1918]

Not surprisingly, this winter cover design incorporates hundreds of snowflakes in this chilly scene. The figure stands before a statue of lovers, itself topped with snow. Her tea rose gown is trimmed with dark fur at the sleeves, waist, and hemline, and a thick fur collar encircles her neck. Her cap, matching the fabric of the coat, is trimmed with braid. A length of fur wraps around her ankle, topped with an artificial tea rose. The background is gray, with spots of white for the snowflakes. [Cover, December 1918]

This figure is surrounded by dolls dressed in authentic costumes from their countries of origin. Their costumes combine white, black, red, and bluish gray. The entire background is purple, the "floor" slightly darker than the walls. The figure's fur-trimmed gown consists of pale and darker orange panels, with a sheer top and a knotted neckpiece. The porthole's border, as well as the roses on the wall, are moss green. The sky outside is pale blue, and the water a darker bluish gray. [Cover, February 1919]

Against a sunburst of yellow and gold, and surrounded by dark and pale gray clouds, this figure dispatches a trail of birds. Her gown and long wrap are of yellow gold and brownish gold with a pattern of abstract designs and floral and bird motifs. Her close-fitting gold cap is attached to her gown in both front and back. She wears gold bracelets on her extended arm. [Cover, March 1919]

Perched on a cliff, surrounded by dandelion fluff, this elegant figure wears a black gown with gray accents. Her long scarf has a pattern of orange shapes on a lighter orange background. She wears a necklace of orange beads on a black strand. Her hair is wrapped in a band of black with orange squares. The plate's background is blue-violet; the cliff is a blend of pale green, brown, orange, and black patches. [Cover, May 1919]

In this early autumn fashions cover plate, the figure is almost lost among the gnarled branches and lush fruit of the sturdy tree. Her pale skin contrasts with the rich poppy red of her draped gown, which encircles the tree trunk beneath her. A few red tendrils of hair frame her sleeping face. The fruit and the lower half of the orb are shades of dark red, the middle background orange, and the top, yellow. The outer part of the plate framing the orb is purple, and the pebbly border is gray. [Cover, Early Autumn Fashions, September 1920]

The applause of the genteel hands shown at the bottom of this cover plate rewards the dancer, who is shown in a garment consisting of gold, orange, and red ribbons. The background color is tomato red. Similarly colored ribbons wrap her legs. The bodice ribbons are gold. Her red hair has been separated into tendrils and decorated with ivory-colored beads. [Cover, Winter Fashions, November 1920]

The orange background and circular patterns and Prussian blue border set off the Art Deco–style figure. The costume consists of a plunging bodice surrounded by a full skirt; the sleeves extend to form a fanciful pattern atop the skirt. The figure wears a spectacular headdress suggesting feathers, as well as an equally extravagant multi-strand necklace. [Cover, February 1921]

This figure, up above the spring flowers in flight from a swarm of insects, wears a floral-patterned skirt; the flowers are a pale red, the larger ones edged in black. The skirt is lined in solid red; her blouse is solid red as well. She grasps the flowing scarf with a black-gloved hand; the scarf's background color is lilac, and the flowers sprinkled on it are the same red as the skirt lining. [Cover, Summer Fashions, May 1921]

Beneath a pale yellow design of fantasy lovers, the dreamer reclines amidst the swirling folds of an enormous robe in brown and rust hues. Strands of pearls accent the garment. The background is a diaphanous pale lavender. The origi-nal plate seems to suggest that the dreamer is part of a large object, such as the planet Earth, and the dreamy disk represents the Sun. [Cover, June 1921]

This figure appears against a lilac-hued fan, which itself is framed by a background of dark orange accented with lighter-orange chrysanthemums. The fan's base has alternating strips of lilac and red. The corner of the fan is yellow with a black button. The costume consists of a multi-tiered flowing gown with a tight-fitting bodice, and a flowing veil. The outer edges of the skirt, as well as the veil, are of light blue, and the background is a lilac hue. Yellow butterflies encircle the figure's head. [Cover, Advance Fall Fashions, September 1921]

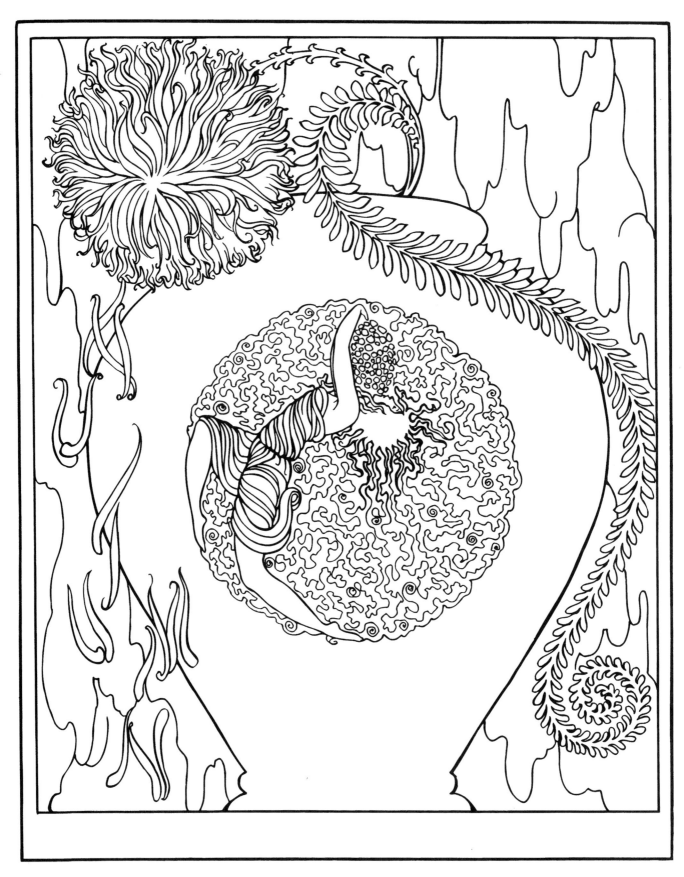

A black vase, seen against a background of reddish browns, contains a figure dressed in a gold draped garment. Her hair is gold and disappears into a swirling gold abstract pattern. Some petals fall from the yellow and orange flower at the top left; its orange stem winds down the side of the vase. The colors are somber, befitting the coming of winter. [Cover, Winter Fashions, November 1921]

Wearing nothing but a "cage" of netting ending in red birds with orange plumage, this light-toned figure appears against a moss green background. Her gown is accented with dark red strands; her headpiece repeats the colors of the birds. The background has splotchy grayish clouds and dark purple patterns resembling bunches of grapes. The reflection consists of lilac swirls on black water, with the gown done in darker hues of the actual colors. The border is reddish-black. [Cover, August 1922]

Left: Bathing costume consisting of contrasting light and dark fabric in a blouson style; the underskirt consists of alternating jagged-edged layers. Worn with a light and dark turban. *Right*: The bathing costume laces at the front and sleeves and is gathered with a broad waistband. Completing the costume are form-fitting leggings in a peacock-eye print. The figure wears a turban-wrapped sunshade. [Illustrations, June 1915]

Shown against a stylized version of Nature (fish swim in the "pond"), this garden costume is made of natural-hued pongee adorned with silk in various colors. The hat can be dropped behind the head by means of ribbons that lace through the upper gown and down through the straw pockets. A white straw garden hat is suspended from the tree; its under-brim of cerise straw mirrors the gown with its laced ribbons. [Illustration, June 1918]

In the window: Fox muff in spiral design *(left)*; tasseled ermine wrap in a scarf style *(right)*. Figure wears coat done in mole skin, upper front and back; the sides of the coat are of a shimmering greenish bronze satin. [Illustration, December 1918]

The gown and the veil of this costume actually are one piece of white mousseline; the front of the gown is drawn back over the head to cover the head and form a flowing train. The sheer fabric is given weight and luster with its intricate silver embroidery. [Illustration, May 1919]

This aviation costume, "Amethyst," is done in a violet wool knit, the blousy shape cinched with a broad laced girdle. The garment top forms a slip-on hood. Two scarves encircle the neck. The soft brown leather gloves and boots have repoussé motifs; the pockets show the same leather motif. [Illustration, September 1920]

The flowing scarf at the left, criss-crossed with the train at the right, mimics the draperies shown in the background of this illustration. *Left:* An ankle-length costume embellished with strands of crystal. *Center:* A turquoise gown with a plunging neckline. The model holds the costume's tasseled belt. A drapery of green satin, with silver stripes, flows from the bodice. *Right:* A violet satin gown with a plunging back. The voluminous train is embroidered with a circular pattern and lined with black velvet. [Illustration, November 1920]

Left: Autumn suit of contrasting hues: beige faced with marine blue moire. Decorative motifs of soutache braid add to the appeal of the design; the braid is also used in the lacings that go through the eyelets. [Illustration, August 1918] *Right*: The extravagantly designed ermine skirt of this costume is topped by a black satin scarf that is wound about the upper body to form a corsage; one end serves as a train. [Illustration, December 1920]

Far left: The back of the garment is pulled forward and fastened at the waistline, giving a Classical appearance. *Center left:* A full cape sweeps backward over the shoulders; figure wears matching striped hat, gloves, and stockings. *Center right:* Boldly striped full-length light-colored robe sweeps over dark gown; the hat repeats the contrasting hues. *Far right:* Long "false" sleeves reveal "bound" sleeves; the gown is fastened with beaded ribbons. [Illustration, March 1921]

Left: Black satin gown with medallion in gold, white, and black embroidery. The design extends into black and white silk cords dotted with gold balls. The girdle catches the upper part of the gown. *Center:* Gray cape with chinchilla bands, lined with coral velvet. Tiny coral beads produce a shoulder medallion. *Right:* Black satin wrap with saffron-hued sleeves; violet and silver embroidery used in sleeve motifs. [Illustration, March 1921]

Flowing full-length drapery with tassels provides a back-drop. [Detail of illustration, November 1918] The figure is dressed in a costume of grayish blue duvetyn with contrast-ing bands of white serge. The cape buttons with a single ivory disk. [Illustration, April 1921]

Left: Dark and light are intertwined in this creation, whose full sleeves are produced by gathering the flowing robe in a twisted waistband. The sleeves are also slit and banded.

Right: This luxurious evening wrap is constructed of gold and lavender velvet, embroidered in silver, gold, and green. [Illustration, April 1921]

The figures are shown against the screen of a marionette theater; the screen is woven into checks using black and white silk. *Left*: Handkerchief-effect evening gown of white, black, and rose silk. *Right*: Layered gown constructed of a single piece of white silk with green lining. [Illustration, September 1921]

Left: Detail of coat constructed of ermine and mole skins in a checkerboard pattern. *Right (and reflection)*: Wrap constructed of two pieces of satin, one black and one white, divided into strips and pulled through gold-embroidered rings. Rolls of black satin strips circle the bolster collar. The color scheme is reversed in the gown. [Illustration, October 1921]

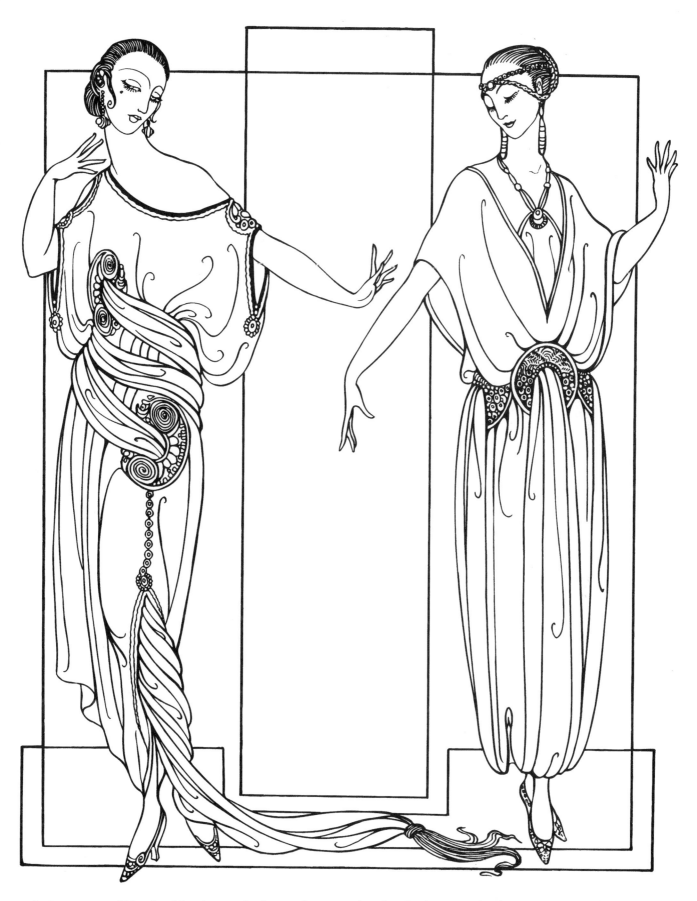

Left: Green satin off-the-shoulder dress with silver embroidery. Girdle of silver tissue, wound about the figure, appears through a front opening to sweep the floor. [Illustration, May 1921] *Right:* A length of green satin, lined with white satin, has been cut into panels; the panels are pulled through embroidered motifs to form a bodice. The gown's edges are stitched with fine silver embroidery. [Illustration, November 1921]

Left: Evening gown of black satin; one end of drapery encircles the wrist, revealing a design done in silver embroidery. [Illustration, May 1921] *Right*: Evening gown constructed of a single piece of cloth, draped and looped about the body. A hand-trained string of pearls is drawn through the gown's girdle. [Illustration, November 1921]

The two figures represent "Evening" and "Night." *Left:* "Evening." Chiffon clouds of grayish blue and grayish purple embellish the orange silk skirt. A setting sun is embroidered on the skirt with gold beads and sparkling diamonds.

Right: A blue veil with dark clouds covers "Night." A pale moon is suggested by the circular pearl headdress. [Illustration, December 1921]

The masked "Fickle Woman" is swathed in a voluminous fur-trimmed wrap; beneath, she wears a ballet-style gown with a narrow, plunging bodice and an exaggeratedly full skirt. [Illustration, February 1922]